The Huge Book of Interesting Facts

by
Jake Jacobs

* * * * *

Published by Jake Jacobs

The Huge Book of Interesting Facts
Copyright© 2023 by Jake Jacobs

1.

Isaac Franks was born on January 21, 1759, in Philadelphia, Pennsylvania.

2.

He came from a prominent Jewish family and was the son of David Franks, a wealthy merchant and military officer.

3.

During the American Revolutionary War, Franks served as an officer in the Continental Army.

4.

He joined the army at the age of 16 and served in various capacities throughout the war.

5.

Franks participated in significant battles, including the Battle of Brandywine and the Battle of Germantown.

6.

He was known for his bravery and leadership skills, quickly rising through the ranks.

7.

Franks served as an aide-de-camp to General Benedict Arnold and played a pivotal role in uncovering Arnold's treasonous plot to surrender West Point to the British.

8.

He was involved in the capture and interrogation of Major John André, the British spy working with Arnold.

9.

Franks's actions helped thwart the plot and preserve the integrity of West Point.

10.

Following the war, Franks continued his military career and achieved the rank of major in the United States Army.

11.

He served as a quartermaster and interpreter, utilizing his language skills in various diplomatic and military assignments.

12.

Franks had a reputation for his linguistic abilities, speaking multiple languages fluently, including French, German, and Hebrew.

13.

He served as an interpreter during negotiations with Native American tribes and in diplomatic interactions with foreign officials.

14.

Franks was involved in the Quasi-War with France in the late 1790s and played a role in defending American interests.

15.

He retired from the military in 1809 and devoted himself to his family and business endeavors.

16.

Franks married Abigail Levy, and they had several children together.

17.

He was an active member of Philadelphia's Jewish community, supporting religious and philanthropic causes.

18.

Franks was a trustee of the University of Pennsylvania and contributed to educational initiatives.

19.

He maintained connections with his fellow Revolutionary War veterans, attending reunions and commemorations.

20.

Franks's military service and contributions were recognized by the Continental Congress, which awarded him a silver medal.

21.

He lived a relatively private life after his retirement from the military and avoided seeking public office.

22.

Franks passed away on November 7, 1822, in Philadelphia at the age of 63.

23.

His legacy as a Jewish military officer during the Revolutionary War highlights the contributions of individuals from diverse backgrounds to the fight for American independence.

24.

Franks's story exemplifies the principles of loyalty, bravery, and dedication to the cause of freedom.

25.

His role in exposing Benedict Arnold's treason showcases his commitment to upholding the values of the newly formed nation.

26.

Franks's life demonstrates the perseverance and accomplishments of Jewish Americans during a time of significant historical transformation.

27.

He is remembered as a courageous soldier who played a crucial part in safeguarding the American cause.

28.

Franks's name is inscribed on the bronze plaques of the Tomb of the Unknown Revolutionary War Soldier in Washington Square, Philadelphia.

29.

His contributions are celebrated by the Jewish community and serve as a source of inspiration for future generations.

30.

Franks's story highlights the importance of inclusivity and the recognition of diverse voices in shaping the nation's history.

31.

He represents the commitment of Jewish Americans to the ideals of religious freedom and equality.

32.

Franks's accomplishments contribute to the broader narrative of the Revolutionary War and the struggle for independence.

33.

His bravery and dedication stand as a testament to the sacrifices made by individuals in the pursuit of liberty and justice.

34.

Franks's military career and involvement in significant historical events underscore the multifaceted nature of the American Revolution.

35.

The memory of Isaac Franks serves as a reminder of the diverse perspectives and contributions that shaped the founding of the United States.

36.

The Chilkoot Trail is a 33-mile (53 km) trail that passes through the Coast Mountains of Alaska and British Columbia.

37.

It was historically used as a trade route by Indigenous people for thousands of years.

38.

The trail gained prominence during the Klondike Gold Rush of 1896-1899.

39.

The Chilkoot Pass, located on the trail, was one of the main routes to the goldfields of the Yukon.

40.

The trail begins in Dyea, Alaska, once a bustling town during the gold rush era, and ends at Bennett, British Columbia.

41.

It takes hikers through diverse landscapes including dense forests, alpine meadows, rocky slopes, and snow-capped mountains.

42.

Hikers can still see remnants of the gold rush era along the trail, including old cabins, artifacts, and tramway systems.

43.

The Chilkoot Trail is managed jointly by Parks Canada and the U.S. National Park Service.

44.

It is designated as a National Historic Site of Canada and a National Historic Landmark in the United States.

45.

The trail is known for its challenging terrain and unpredictable weather conditions, including heavy rain, snow, and high winds.

46.

Hiking the Chilkoot Trail requires a permit, and only a limited number of permits are issued each year to manage the trail's impact.

47.

The trail is popular among outdoor enthusiasts and history buffs, attracting hikers from around the world.

48.

It offers breathtaking views of surrounding mountains, glaciers, and pristine wilderness.

49.

The Chilkoot Trail is home to a variety of wildlife, including bears, moose, eagles, and mountain goats.

50.

Hikers may encounter challenging river crossings, particularly at the Taiya and Happy Camp sections.

51.

The trail's highest point is the Chilkoot Pass, standing at an elevation of 3,759 feet (1,146 meters).

52.

The pass is marked by the famous "Golden Stairs," a steep and challenging ascent of about 1,000 steps.

53.

The trail passes by several historic campsites, such as Sheep Camp, Lindeman City, and Bennett City.

54.

Hikers can still find remnants of old pack trails and staircases built during the gold rush era.

55.

The Chilkoot Trail is rich in cultural history, with stories of Indigenous people, gold prospectors, and early settlers.

56.

The trail is often hiked in multiple days, with designated campgrounds along the route.

57.

The Chilkoot Trail offers opportunities for fishing, birdwatching, and photography.

58.

Hikers need to be self-sufficient and carry all their food and camping gear, as there are no services or facilities along the trail.

59.

The trail can be physically demanding, requiring good physical fitness and proper gear.

60.

Several books and documentaries have been written about the Chilkoot Trail and its historical significance.

61.

The Chilkoot Trail has been featured in movies and TV shows, including the popular miniseries "Klondike" (2014).

62.

The trail is part of the larger Klondike Gold Rush National Historical Park, which preserves and interprets the gold rush history.

63.

The Chilkoot Trail is considered a pilgrimage for many hikers, offering a unique connection to the past and the spirit of adventure.

64.

The trail can be hiked in either direction, but most hikers start from Dyea and finish in Bennett.

65.

The Chilkoot Trail is well-marked with trail signs and markers, making navigation relatively straightforward.

66.

It is recommended to hike the trail during the summer months, between June and September, when the weather is more favorable.

67.

The Chilkoot Trail requires hikers to pack out all their garbage and follow Leave No Trace principles to preserve the wilderness.

68.

The trail provides an opportunity to learn about the challenges and hardships faced by gold rush prospectors in the late 19th century.

69.

Hikers can see remnants of the Klondike Gold Rush, such as discarded mining equipment and artifacts.

70.

The Chilkoot Trail offers a sense of solitude and remoteness, allowing hikers to disconnect from the modern world.

71.

The trail has a rich cultural significance for the local Indigenous communities, who continue to maintain a strong connection to the land.

72.

Hikers can experience a sense of accomplishment upon completing the challenging trail, reminiscent of the perseverance shown by gold rush prospectors.

73.

The Chilkoot Trail has been the subject of artistic works, including paintings, photographs, and literary works.

74.

The trail is known for its wildflowers, with vibrant displays of colors during the summer months.

75.

The Chilkoot Trail provides a glimpse into the harsh conditions endured by gold rush stampeders, including extreme cold and avalanches.

76.

Hikers are advised to be prepared for encounters with bears and follow proper safety precautions.

77.

The Chilkoot Trail has designated bear caches where hikers can safely store their food to avoid attracting wildlife.

78.

The trail offers a chance to forge lasting friendships and camaraderie among fellow hikers, sharing the challenges and joys of the journey.

79.

Hikers can experience the unique sensation of stepping back in time as they traverse the same path as gold rush prospectors.

80.

The Chilkoot Trail showcases the resilience and determination of those who sought their fortune in the Klondike goldfields.

81.

The trail offers a blend of natural beauty, human history, and adventure, making it a memorable experience for hikers.

82.

Hiking the Chilkoot Trail requires careful planning and preparation, including obtaining permits, arranging transportation, and studying trail conditions.

83.

The Chilkoot Trail crosses the boundary between the United States and Canada, requiring hikers to carry proper identification.

84.

The trail's remoteness and untouched landscapes provide a sense of tranquility and serenity, away from the hustle and bustle of modern life.

85.

The Chilkoot Trail offers a connection to the past and a deeper appreciation for the natural and historical wonders of the region.

86.

Elbridge Gerry was born on July 17, 1744, in Marblehead, Massachusetts.

87.

He came from a prosperous merchant family and received a quality education.

88.

Gerry graduated from Harvard College in 1762 at the age of 18.

89.

He was involved in trade and became successful in the shipping industry.

90.

Gerry married Ann Thompson in 1765, and they had ten children together.

91.

He was a delegate to the Continental Congress from 1776 to 1780.

92.

Gerry signed the Declaration of Independence in 1776, representing Massachusetts.

93.

He was an advocate for states' rights and limited central government power.

94.

Gerry served as a member of the Massachusetts Constitutional Convention in 1779-1780.

95.

He played a key role in drafting the Massachusetts Constitution, which served as a model for the U.S. Constitution.

96.

Gerry was opposed to the original draft of the U.S. Constitution and did not sign it at the Constitutional Convention in 1787.

97.

He believed that the Constitution did not adequately protect individual liberties and feared an overly powerful central government.

98.

Gerry eventually became a supporter of the Constitution after the addition of the Bill of Rights.

99.

Gerry served as the fifth Vice President of the United States from 1813 until his death in 1814.

100.

He was Vice President under President James Madison.

101.

Gerry is best known for his role in the political controversy surrounding gerrymandering.

102.

The term "gerrymander" was coined based on Gerry's actions as Governor of Massachusetts, where he approved a controversial redistricting plan in 1812.

103.

Gerry's redistricting plan was criticized for creating oddly shaped districts to benefit his political party.

104.

Gerry's redistricting plan was caricatured as a salamander in a political cartoon, giving rise to the term "gerrymander."

105.

Gerry served as the Governor of Massachusetts from 1810 to 1812.

106.

As Governor, Gerry worked to improve education and promote economic growth in the state.

107.

He was a strong advocate for religious freedom and fought against religious discrimination.

108.

Gerry supported the abolitionist movement and was active in the fight against slavery.

109.

He was one of the founding members of the American Antislavery Society.

110.

Gerry was a member of the Democratic-Republican Party, which was led by Thomas Jefferson and James Madison.

111.

He was known for his strong support of Jeffersonian principles and limited government.

112.

Gerry was an influential figure in Massachusetts politics, serving in various positions throughout his career.

113.

He was a delegate to the Massachusetts Provincial Congress and later served in the Massachusetts House of Representatives.

114.

Gerry was also a member of the Massachusetts Senate.

115.

He played a crucial role in the formation of the United States Navy, advocating for its establishment.

116.

Gerry was a proponent of diplomatic negotiations and believed in resolving conflicts peacefully.

117.

He served as a diplomat and was sent on several diplomatic missions, including to France and Spain.

118.

Gerry was known for his frugal lifestyle and simple tastes, despite his family's wealth.

119.

He was a committed public servant and dedicated much of his life to serving his country and his state.

120.

Gerry was well-respected for his intelligence, integrity, and dedication to principles.

121.

He was known for his strong sense of duty and willingness to make difficult decisions.

122.

Gerry's health declined in the later years of his life, and he passed away on November 23, 1814, at the age of 70.

123.

He is buried in the Congressional Cemetery in Washington, D.C.

124.

Gerry's legacy is tied to his contributions to the early development of American democracy.

125.

He played a crucial role in the formation of the nation and the establishment of democratic institutions.

126.

Gerry's name is associated with the concept of gerrymandering, which continues to be a topic of political debate to this day.

127.

Despite his initial reservations, Gerry became an ardent supporter of the Constitution and worked to ensure the protection of individual liberties.

128.

Gerry's stance on states' rights and limited government power continues to resonate with advocates of decentralized governance.

129.

He was a firm believer in the importance of citizen participation in government and the need for regular elections.

130.

Gerry's contributions to the fight against slavery and his support for religious freedom reflect his commitment to human rights and equality.

131.

His role in shaping the Massachusetts Constitution demonstrates his dedication to creating a just and fair system of government.

132.

Gerry's intellectual prowess and political acumen made him a respected figure among his peers.

133.

He was a skilled negotiator and was able to build consensus among disparate groups.

134.

Gerry's commitment to public service and his tireless advocacy for the principles he believed in left a lasting impact on American politics.

135.

His contributions to the early years of the United States helped shape the nation and set the course for its democratic future.

136.

Hedgehogs are small, nocturnal mammals known for their spiky coat of quills.

137.

There are 17 species of hedgehogs found in Europe, Asia, and Africa.

138.

Hedgehogs are primarily insectivores, but they may also eat small vertebrates, eggs, fruits, and fungi.

139.

They have excellent hearing and a strong sense of smell, which helps them locate prey.

140.

Hedgehogs are solitary animals and prefer to live alone, except during mating season.

141.

They are known for their ability to roll into a tight ball when threatened, with their spines providing protection.

142.

Hedgehogs have about 5,000 to 7,000 spines on their back, which are modified hairs made of keratin.

143.

Contrary to popular belief, hedgehogs cannot shoot their quills.

144.

Hedgehogs are excellent climbers and can also swim.

145.

They have relatively poor eyesight but compensate with their other senses.

146.

Hedgehogs are immune to certain snake venoms, allowing them to eat venomous snakes.

147.

They communicate through a range of vocalizations, including hissing, grunting, and snuffling sounds.

148.

Hedgehogs have a long lifespan for their size, with some living up to 10 years or more in captivity.

149.

Their spines are not poisonous or barbed, but they can be sharp and cause discomfort if mishandled.

150.

Hedgehogs go through a process called "self-anointing," where they produce frothy saliva and spread it on their spines.

151.

This behavior is believed to help camouflage their scent and potentially deter predators.

152.

Hedgehogs are prone to obesity if overfed, so a balanced diet is crucial for their health.

153.

They have a high tolerance for cold temperatures and can hibernate during the winter.

154.

Hedgehogs are natural pest controllers, as they eat insects and help keep populations in check.

155.

Their natural predators include foxes, owls, and larger birds of prey.

156.

Hedgehogs have a relatively low body temperature, typically ranging between 86 to 99 degrees Fahrenheit.

157.

They have a strong immune system and are rarely affected by diseases or parasites.

158.

Hedgehogs have a unique gait known as "hedgehog waddle," where they shuffle their feet as they walk.

159.

They have a good sense of direction and can navigate their surroundings using landmarks and scent trails.

160.

Hedgehogs are crepuscular, meaning they are most active during twilight hours.

161.

They have a remarkable ability to curl into a tight ball within seconds when they sense danger.

162.

Hedgehogs have a keen sense of balance and can walk along narrow ledges without falling.

163.

They have a specialized stomach adapted to break down the exoskeletons of insects.

164.

Hedgehogs have a unique defense mechanism where they produce a foul-smelling odor from their anal glands.

165.

They are efficient diggers and use their strong front paws and sharp claws to burrow and create nests.

166.

Hedgehogs have a preference for open grasslands, woodlands, and gardens as their natural habitats.

167.

They are not related to porcupines or echidnas, despite the similar appearance of spines.

168.

Hedgehogs are born blind and deaf, relying on their sense of smell and touch to navigate their environment.

169.

Baby hedgehogs, called hoglets, are born with soft spines that harden within a few hours.

170.

Hedgehogs are known for their ability to roll onto their backs and expose their vulnerable bellies when relaxed.

171.

They have a small, black nose and round, black eyes, which are well-adapted for their nocturnal lifestyle.

172.

Hedgehogs are naturally curious animals and may investigate new objects or scents in their environment.

173.

They are skilled swimmers and can paddle across water bodies when necessary.

174.

Hedgehogs are surprisingly fast runners and can reach speeds of up to 6 miles per hour.

175.

They are meticulous groomers and use their tongue to clean their spines and remove debris.

176.

Hedgehogs have a high tolerance for pain and can endure minor injuries without showing signs of distress.

177.

They have a unique dental structure, with sharp incisors and molars adapted for crushing and grinding food.

178.

Hedgehogs are known to exhibit territorial behavior and mark their territory with urine.

179.

They have a relatively low metabolic rate, which allows them to conserve energy during periods of food scarcity.

180.

Hedgehogs have a complex mating ritual that involves various courtship displays and vocalizations.

181.

Female hedgehogs typically give birth to a litter of 4 to 6 hoglets, which are cared for by the mother.

182.

Hedgehogs have been domesticated as pets in some countries but require specific care and diet to thrive.

183.

They are naturally resistant to many common pests, such as fleas and ticks, due to their spiky coat..

184.

Hedgehogs are protected by law in many countries, as they are considered a valuable part of the ecosystem.

185.

They have captured the hearts of many people around the world with their adorable appearance and unique behaviors.

186.

Aardvarks are nocturnal mammals native to Africa.

187.

They are the only living species in the order Tubulidentata.

188.

Aardvarks are known for their long, tubular snouts, which they use to sniff out insects.

189.

Their name comes from the Afrikaans word "aardvark," which means "earth pig."

190.

Aardvarks have a unique dental structure with peg-like teeth and no enamel.

191.

They rely on their powerful claws to dig burrows in search of food and for shelter.

192.

Aardvarks are excellent diggers and can create complex underground tunnels.

193.

Their burrows can be as long as 13 meters (43 feet) and have multiple entrances.

194.

Aardvarks are solitary animals and are most commonly seen alone.

195.

They have large, sticky tongues that can extend up to 30 centimeters (12 inches) to capture insects.

196.

Aardvarks primarily feed on ants and termites, consuming thousands of them in a single night.

197.

They use their strong front legs and claws to break into termite mounds and ant hills.

198.

Aardvarks have poor eyesight but compensate with a keen sense of smell and hearing.

199.

They have long, rabbit-like ears that can move independently to detect sounds.

200.

Aardvarks have a thick skin that protects them from insect bites and can withstand thorny vegetation.

201.

Despite their appearance, aardvarks are not related to pigs. They belong to their own unique family.

202.

Aardvarks are capable swimmers and can cross bodies of water when necessary.

203.

They are known for their slow and deliberate movements on land.

204.

Aardvarks have a specialized digestive system to process their insect-based diet.

205.

They can eat up to 50,000 insects in a single night, helping to control insect populations.

206.

Aardvarks have a gestation period of about 7 months and typically give birth to one offspring.

207.

The young aardvark, called a cub, remains in the burrow for the first few weeks of its life.

208.

Aardvark cubs have a lighter fur color, which darkens as they grow older.

209.

They reach sexual maturity around 2 to 3 years of age.

210.

Aardvarks are not aggressive animals and will generally retreat when confronted by a threat.

211.

They can defend themselves by using their strong claws and powerful tails to strike attackers.

212.

Aardvarks are preyed upon by large carnivores, such as lions, hyenas, and leopards.

213.

They have a unique defense mechanism known as "aardvark ballet," where they rapidly twist and turn to confuse predators.

214.

Aardvarks are considered keystone species as their burrows provide shelter for other animals.

215.

Their burrows are used by other creatures like warthogs, mongoose, and reptiles.

216.

Aardvarks are skilled at camouflage and can blend into their surroundings with their sandy-colored fur.

217.

They are known to make soft grunting or hissing sounds as a form of communication.

218.

Aardvarks have a lifespan of around 10 to 15 years in the wild.

219.

In captivity, they can live up to 23 years.

220.

Aardvarks are excellent excavators and can clear large areas of land while searching for food.

221.

They have a thick skin that helps protect them from insect bites and the sun's rays.

222.

Aardvarks have a keen sense of smell, which helps them locate insect colonies underground.

223.

They have relatively poor vision, relying more on their sense of smell and hearing.

224.

Aardvarks have a long, sticky tongue that can extend up to 30 centimeters (12 inches) to catch insects.

225.

The tongue is covered in mucus, which helps trap the insects and pull them into the mouth.

226.

Aardvarks are known for their powerful claws, which they use for digging burrows and breaking open termite mounds.

227.

They can dig burrows as deep as 2 meters (6.6 feet) and as long as 13 meters (43 feet).

228.

Aardvarks are generally solitary animals, but they may tolerate the presence of other aardvarks in their territory.

229.

They mark their territory with urine and scent secretions from their anal glands.

230.

Aardvarks have a unique mating behavior where the male chases the female and engages in a wrestling match before mating.

231.

The female gives birth to a single cub after a gestation period of about 7 months.

232.

The mother nurses the cub for several months before introducing it to solid food.

233.

Aardvarks are considered vulnerable to extinction due to habitat loss and poaching.

234.

They play an important role in the ecosystem by controlling termite and ant populations.

235.

Aardvarks have captivated the interest of researchers and the public with their unique adaptations and fascinating behavior.

236.

Stephen Girard was born on May 20, 1750, in Bordeaux, France.

237.

He came from a humble background and worked as a cabin boy on a merchant ship before immigrating to America.

238.

Girard settled in Philadelphia, Pennsylvania, where he became a prominent businessman and banker.

239.

He played a crucial role in financing the American government during the War of 1812.

240.

Girard amassed a significant fortune through various business ventures, including shipping, trade, and real estate.

241.

He established the first fully steam-powered cotton mill in America.

242.

Girard's philanthropic efforts were extensive. He donated vast sums of money to various charitable causes.

243.

He provided financial support to numerous institutions, including hospitals, orphanages, and schools.

244.

Girard College, a Philadelphia-based boarding school for orphaned children, was founded and funded by Stephen Girard.

245.

He made substantial contributions to the development of the city of Philadelphia, including the construction of several buildings and infrastructure projects.

246.

Girard was known for his strict business practices and attention to detail.

247.

Despite his wealth, he led a relatively modest and frugal lifestyle.

248.

Girard was a private individual and kept a low public profile.

249.

He never married or had any children of his own.

250.

Girard was deeply committed to education and believed in providing opportunities for underprivileged children.

251.

He specified in his will that his assets should be used to establish a college for orphaned boys, which eventually became Girard College.

252.

Girard College was one of the first educational institutions to admit students regardless of race, a progressive stance at the time.

253.

Girard's will was highly detailed and included specific instructions on how his assets should be managed and used after his death.

254.

He left the bulk of his estate to Girard College, making it one of the wealthiest educational institutions in the United States.

255.

Girard's legacy as a philanthropist and entrepreneur continues to impact countless lives to this day.

256.

He played a pivotal role in the development of Philadelphia's shipping industry, making the city a major maritime center.

257.

Girard was a shrewd investor and had a keen understanding of finance and commerce.

258.

During the yellow fever epidemic of 1793 in Philadelphia, Girard courageously took charge of relief efforts, converting his own home into a hospital.

259.

He personally cared for the sick and dying during the epidemic, demonstrating compassion and dedication.

260.

Girard became one of the wealthiest individuals in America during his lifetime.

261.

He played a significant role in the growth of the United States as an economic power.

262.

Girard's business empire extended beyond the United States, with trade connections across the globe.

263.

He owned a fleet of ships that traversed the Atlantic and engaged in international trade.

264.

Girard was known for his meticulous record-keeping and financial acumen.

265.

He was a strong advocate for free trade and economic growth.

266.

Girard's financial contributions helped stabilize the U.S. economy during times of crisis, including the Panic of 1819.

267.

He founded the Girard Bank, which later merged with other institutions to become Girard Bank & Trust.

268.

Girard was an ardent supporter of the American Revolution and actively participated in the war effort.

269.

He supplied ships and provisions to the Continental Army, playing a crucial role in the success of the American cause.

270.

Girard was a firm believer in self-reliance and hard work, principles he applied to his own life and encouraged in others.

271.

He was a staunch advocate for the rights of workers and ensured fair treatment and reasonable wages for his employees.

272.

Girard's business empire extended beyond commerce and banking. He also had interests in coal mining and canal construction.

273.

Despite facing personal tragedies, including the deaths of several family members, Girard persevered and continued to build his fortune.

274.

He was known for his astute negotiation skills and ability to strike profitable deals.

275.

Girard's dedication to education extended beyond Girard College. He supported other educational initiatives and scholarships.

276.

He was an early supporter of public education and believed in the importance of providing accessible schooling to all children.

277.

Girard's success as a businessman and philanthropist was driven by his strong work ethic and unwavering determination.

278.

He maintained a vast network of business connections and cultivated relationships with influential individuals.

279.

Girard's contributions to Philadelphia's growth and development were recognized and celebrated during his lifetime.

280.

He was regarded as one of the most influential and respected figures in the city.

281.

Girard's impact on education and philanthropy in the United States inspired others to follow in his footsteps.

282.

His estate and legacy continue to be carefully managed, ensuring the ongoing support of Girard College and the causes he championed.

283.

Girard's life and achievements have been the subject of numerous books, articles, and scholarly studies.

284.

His story serves as a testament to the transformative power of hard work, perseverance, and the belief in the value of education.

285.

Stephen Girard's name is forever intertwined with the history of Philadelphia and the legacy of philanthropy in the United States.

286.

Nathanael Greene was born on August 7, 1742, in Warwick, Rhode Island.

287.

He played a crucial role in the American Revolutionary War and is considered one of the most skilled and strategic generals of the Continental Army.

288.

Greene began his military career as a private in the Kentish Guards, a Rhode Island militia unit.

289.

He quickly rose through the ranks due to his leadership abilities and tactical acumen.

290.

Greene served as a quartermaster general in the early stages of the war, responsible for managing the army's supplies and logistics.

291.

He played a key role in reorganizing the Continental Army and improving its efficiency.

292.

Greene developed a close working relationship with General George Washington, who recognized his military prowess.

293.

Greene's military strategy focused on guerrilla warfare, hit-and-run tactics, and avoiding direct confrontation with the more powerful British forces.

294.

He was known for his ability to adapt to changing circumstances and make quick decisions on the battlefield.

295.

Greene is best known for his leadership during the Southern Campaign, where he effectively outmaneuvered and wore down the British forces in the southern colonies.

296.

Despite initial setbacks, Greene's strategic brilliance helped turn the tide of the war in the South in favor of the Patriots.

297.

He successfully utilized a strategy of attrition, avoiding large-scale battles while wearing down the British through small-scale engagements and harassment.

298.

Greene's leadership and tactical skills were instrumental in the American victories at the battles of Cowpens and Guilford Courthouse.

299.

He demonstrated exceptional military leadership in his ability to coordinate and command diverse militia and Continental Army units.

300.

Greene's efforts in the South forced the British to shift their focus away from the northern colonies and eventually contributed to their ultimate defeat.

301.

After the war, Greene retired from military service and settled in Georgia, where he became involved in politics and business.

302.

He served as the Governor of Rhode Island from 1786 to 1790.

303.

Greene was a proponent of a strong central government and played a significant role in advocating for the ratification of the United States Constitution.

304.

He strongly opposed the institution of slavery and made efforts to promote its abolition in his home state of Rhode Island.

305.

Greene's military accomplishments earned him the nickname "The Fighting Quaker" due to his Quaker upbringing.

306.

He was known for his humility, integrity, and dedication to the principles of liberty and independence.

307.

Greene was highly respected by his troops and fellow officers for his fairness and compassion.

308.

He believed in the importance of training and discipline, and his soldiers admired his commitment to their welfare and well-being.

309.

Greene's military strategies and tactics continue to be studied by military historians and strategists.

310.

He wrote several important military treatises, including "The Greene Papers" and "Observations on the Siege of Ninety-Six."

311.

Greene's legacy as a military leader has had a lasting impact on the development of the United States Army and its strategies.

312.

He advocated for a strong and professional standing army to defend the nation and protect its interests.

313.

Greene's contributions to the American Revolution are celebrated and recognized through various memorials, including the Nathanael Greene Monument in Savannah, Georgia.

314.

In 2008, Greene was posthumously awarded the Order of the Palmetto, the highest civilian honor in South Carolina.

315.

Greene's birthplace, the Nathanael Greene Homestead, is now a National Historic Landmark and museum.

316.

Greene's military career spanned from 1774 to 1783, with his service to the cause of American independence.

317.

He participated in many key battles of the American Revolution, including the Battle of Bunker Hill and the Battle of Trenton.

318.

Greene's military strategy emphasized the importance of mobility, surprise, and the use of local militia.

319.

He believed in the value of training and discipline and emphasized the need for a well-drilled and professional army.

320.

Greene's leadership style was characterized by his ability to inspire his troops through example and personal courage.

321.

He was known for his strategic vision and his ability to anticipate and respond to enemy movements.

322.

Greene was involved in the planning and execution of the pivotal Battle of Saratoga, which is considered a turning point in the war.

323.

He played a crucial role in the formation of the Society of the Cincinnati, a fraternal organization of Revolutionary War officers.

324.

Greene's military genius and contributions to the war effort earned him the respect and admiration of his contemporaries, including George Washington and Thomas Jefferson.

325.

He was an advocate for the professionalization of the military and the establishment of a military academy, which later led to the founding of the United States Military Academy at West Point.

326.

Greene's legacy as a military leader extends beyond the American Revolution. His strategic thinking and innovative tactics have influenced military leaders throughout history.

327.

Greene's writings on military tactics and strategy continue to be studied and referenced by military scholars and historians.

<h1 style="text-align:center">328.</h1>

He was posthumously awarded the Purple Heart in 1932 for his service and sacrifices during the American Revolution.

<h1 style="text-align:center">329.</h1>

Greene's statue stands prominently in Lafayette Park in Washington, D.C., as a tribute to his contributions to the nation.

<h1 style="text-align:center">330.</h1>

Greene's military achievements were not limited to the battlefield. He also played a crucial role in establishing logistical systems to support the army's operations.

<h1 style="text-align:center">331.</h1>

He is considered one of the founding fathers of the United States and a key figure in the successful fight for independence.

<h1 style="text-align:center">332.</h1>

Greene's contributions to the war effort were instrumental in securing the freedoms and liberties that Americans enjoy today.

<h1 style="text-align:center">333.</h1>

His legacy as a military leader and patriot is celebrated every year on Nathanael Greene Day, observed on August 7th, his birthday.

<h1 style="text-align:center">334.</h1>

Greene's strategic brilliance and leadership skills continue to inspire military leaders and scholars around the world.

<h1 style="text-align:center">335.</h1>

His life and accomplishments serve as a reminder of the indomitable spirit and unwavering commitment to freedom that fueled the American Revolution.

336.

The Church of the Holy Ascension is a historic church located in the village of Ascension, near Pittsburgh, Pennsylvania.

337.

The church was built in 1889 and is one of the oldest standing structures in the area.

338.

It is a fine example of Gothic Revival architecture, with its distinctive pointed arches, stained glass windows, and intricate stone carvings.

339.

The church was originally built to serve the growing community of coal miners and their families in the area.

340.

The construction of the church was funded by local residents and the coal mining company.

341.

The Church of the Holy Ascension is affiliated with the Episcopal Church and continues to be an active place of worship.

342.

The church's design and architecture were inspired by medieval European cathedrals, giving it a grand and majestic appearance.

343.

The interior of the church features beautiful stained glass windows depicting biblical scenes and saints.

344.

The church's bell tower houses a historic bell that has been in use since the church was built.

345.

The Church of the Holy Ascension has a strong sense of community and has been a gathering place for generations of families in the area.

346.

Over the years, the church has played a significant role in the lives of its parishioners, hosting weddings, baptisms, and funerals.

347.

The church's cemetery is the final resting place for many of the area's early settlers and community members.

348.

The Church of the Holy Ascension is known for its vibrant music program, including a choir that performs during services and special events.

349.

The church's pipe organ is a centerpiece of its music program and has been played by accomplished organists throughout its history.

350.

The church has undergone several renovations and restorations over the years to preserve its historic beauty and structural integrity.

351.

The church's interior features intricate woodwork, including hand-carved pews and a beautifully crafted altar.

352.

The Church of the Holy Ascension is listed on the National Register
of Historic Places, recognizing its architectural and historical
significance.

353.

The church's stained glass windows were crafted by renowned
artisans, using vibrant colors and intricate details to create
breathtaking visual displays.

354.

The church's annual Christmas Eve service is a cherished tradition in
the community, drawing large crowds of worshippers.

355.

The church actively participates in community outreach programs,
providing support and assistance to those in need.

356.

The Church of the Holy Ascension is a hub for cultural and
educational events, hosting concerts, lectures, and art exhibitions.

357.

The church's clergy and congregation have been actively involved in
local charitable initiatives, supporting causes such as food banks,
shelters, and educational programs.

358.

The church's stunning architecture and serene atmosphere make it a
popular venue for weddings, attracting couples from near and far.

359.

The Church of the Holy Ascension has a strong commitment to
environmental stewardship and has implemented sustainable
practices in its operations.

360.

The church's annual Easter sunrise service, held on the church grounds, is a cherished tradition that brings the community together to celebrate the resurrection.

361.

The church organizes regular educational and spiritual development programs for its members, including Bible studies, prayer groups, and retreats.

362.

The church has a rich history of community involvement and activism, advocating for social justice and equality.

363.

The Church of the Holy Ascension's architecture and serene surroundings provide a peaceful sanctuary for meditation and reflection.

364.

The church's vibrant stained glass windows create a kaleidoscope of colors when the sunlight streams through them.

365.

The church's sanctuary is adorned with beautiful floral arrangements during special celebrations and holidays.

366.

The church's outdoor grounds feature well-maintained gardens and landscaping, providing a tranquil setting for contemplation.

367.

The Church of the Holy Ascension has a dedicated team of volunteers who assist with various church activities and programs.

368.

The church's annual harvest festival is a joyous event that celebrates the abundance of the harvest season and brings the community together.

369.

The church has an active youth group that organizes social and service-oriented activities for young members of the congregation.

370.

The church hosts regular concerts and musical performances, showcasing local talent and fostering a love for the arts.

371.

The Church of the Holy Ascension has a deep sense of history and heritage, preserving its archives and artifacts for future generations.

372.

The church's stained glass windows are not only visually stunning but also tell stories from the Bible, providing a source of inspiration for worshippers.

373.

The church's location, nestled amidst scenic surroundings, offers a peaceful retreat away from the hustle and bustle of everyday life.

374.

The church's clergy are known for their compassionate and inclusive approach, welcoming people from all walks of life.

375.

The Church of the Holy Ascension has a strong commitment to interfaith dialogue and cooperation, fostering understanding and unity among different religious communities.

376.

The church's annual Thanksgiving service incorporates traditions from various cultural backgrounds, highlighting the diversity of its congregation.

377.

The church's roof is adorned with intricate architectural details, including finials, gargoyles, and ornamental motifs.

378.

The Church of the Holy Ascension's weekly services feature engaging sermons that address contemporary issues and provide guidance for spiritual growth.

379.

The church's community outreach extends beyond its immediate vicinity, supporting global initiatives for humanitarian aid and disaster relief.

380.

The church's interior is adorned with exquisite artwork, including religious paintings and sculptures, creating a sacred atmosphere.

381.

The Church of the Holy Ascension has a strong commitment to preserving the natural environment, implementing eco-friendly practices in its operations.

382.

The church's Sunday school program offers engaging and age-appropriate educational activities for children, instilling important values and teachings.

383.

The church's stained glass windows were carefully restored during a recent renovation, bringing back their original splendor.

384.

The Church of the Holy Ascension continues to be a spiritual beacon in the community, providing a place of solace, worship, and fellowship for all who enter its doors.

385.

The Eagle Historic District is located in Eagle, Colorado, USA.

386.

It is listed on the National Register of Historic Places.

387.

The district encompasses the downtown area of Eagle, which is known for its well-preserved historic buildings.

388.

The district features a mix of architectural styles, including Victorian, Italianate, and Queen Anne.

389.

Many of the buildings in the district date back to the late 19th and early 20th centuries.

390.

The district's architectural heritage reflects the town's development as a trading and ranching center.

391.

The Eagle Historic District is characterized by its charming and walkable streets lined with historic buildings.

392.

It showcases the town's rich history and cultural heritage.

393.

The district is a popular destination for history buffs and architecture enthusiasts.

394.

It offers a glimpse into the town's past, showcasing its growth and development over time.

395.

The district is home to several notable buildings, including the historic Eagle County Courthouse.

396.

The courthouse is an impressive two-story brick building constructed in 1924.

397.

The district features a variety of commercial buildings, including old storefronts and shops.

398.

Many of these buildings have been repurposed as restaurants, boutiques, and art galleries.

399.

The district also includes residential structures, such as charming Victorian homes.

400.

Some of the homes in the district have been converted into bed and breakfasts or guesthouses.

401.

The district's architecture reflects the influence of the mining industry on the town's development.

402.

Eagle was once a hub for mining activities, particularly silver and lead mining.

403.

The historic district showcases the town's transition from a mining center to a vibrant community.

404.

It serves as a reminder of the town's resilience and adaptability.

405.

The district is surrounded by stunning natural beauty, with the Rocky Mountains as its backdrop.

406.

Visitors can enjoy scenic views and outdoor activities in the nearby Eagle River and White River National Forest.

407.

The district hosts several events and festivals throughout the year, celebrating the town's heritage.

408.

It is a lively and bustling area, with a vibrant local community.

409.

The district has been carefully preserved and maintained, thanks to the efforts of local preservation organizations.

410.

It offers walking tours and guided visits for visitors to explore and learn about its history.

411.

The district's buildings feature unique architectural details, such as ornate facades and decorative elements.

412.

Some of the buildings have plaques or markers that provide historical information.

413.

The district has served as a backdrop for film and television productions due to its picturesque charm.

414.

It has been featured in various movies, showcasing its authentic small-town atmosphere.

415.

The district is a popular spot for photographers, artists, and history researchers.

416.

It offers a wealth of inspiration and opportunities for capturing the town's character.

417.

The district's streets are lined with mature trees, providing shade and a pleasant ambiance.

418.

It is a pedestrian-friendly area, with wide sidewalks and crosswalks.

419.

The district is conveniently located near amenities such as shops, restaurants, and accommodations.

420.

It serves as a gathering place for the local community, hosting events and celebrations.

421.

The district has been recognized for its preservation efforts and commitment to historic integrity.

422.

It contributes to the overall identity and sense of place of Eagle.

423.

The district is a living testament to the town's past and a reflection of its values and traditions.

424.

It attracts visitors from near and far, contributing to the local economy.

425.

The district's buildings have unique stories and histories associated with them.

426.

Some of the buildings have undergone restoration and adaptive reuse projects to maintain their relevance.

427.

The district's architecture reflects the craftsmanship and architectural styles prevalent during its construction.

428.

It offers opportunities for exploring local businesses, including boutique shops and eateries.

429.

The district is a vibrant and dynamic place, with a mix of old and new establishments.

430.

It is a hub for community gatherings and cultural events, fostering a sense of belonging and pride.

431.

The district's architecture and streetscape create a charming and nostalgic atmosphere.

432.

It provides a glimpse into the daily life and activities of the town's early residents.

433.

The district is a testament to the importance of preserving and celebrating historic places.

434.

It continues to play a significant role in shaping the identity and character of Eagle, Colorado.

435.

Button Gwinnett was born on April 10, 1735, in Down Hatherley, Gloucestershire, England.

436.

He was the third of seven children born to Reverend Samuel Gwinnett and Anne Gwinnett.

437.

Gwinnett's family had Welsh origins and migrated to England from Wales.

438.

He received his education at the College of William and Mary in Virginia.

439.

Gwinnett initially pursued a career as a merchant and later became a plantation owner in Georgia.

440.

In 1765, he moved to Savannah, Georgia, where he became involved in local politics.

441.

Gwinnett was an outspoken supporter of American independence from Britain.

442.

He played a significant role in the American Revolutionary War and the formation of the new nation.

443.

Gwinnett was elected to the Provincial Congress of Georgia in 1776.

444.

He was one of three Georgians to sign the United States Declaration of Independence on July 4, 1776.

445.

Gwinnett's signature on the Declaration of Independence is highly sought after by collectors, making it one of the rarest and most valuable autographs.

446.

He served as the Speaker of the Georgia Assembly and as the president of Georgia's Council of Safety.

447.

Gwinnett was appointed as a brigadier general in the Georgia militia and was tasked with defending the state against British forces.

448.

He played a crucial role in the Battle of the Rice Boats, a successful American operation against the British in 1776.

449.

Gwinnett's efforts to strengthen Georgia's military forces were instrumental in the defense of the state.

450.

Gwinnett's political career was marked by conflict and rivalry with fellow Georgian Lachlan McIntosh.

451.

The rivalry escalated to a duel in 1777, in which Gwinnett was wounded.

452.

Following the duel, Gwinnett's influence and popularity began to decline.

453.

He lost his bid for re-election to the Georgia Assembly in 1777, effectively ending his political career.

454.

Gwinnett turned his attention to business ventures, including land speculation and trading.

455.

He suffered financial difficulties and accumulated significant debts.

456.

Gwinnett's financial struggles led to legal disputes and lawsuits.

457.

In 1779, Gwinnett challenged Lachlan McIntosh to a second duel, but this time Gwinnett was fatally wounded and died on May 19, 1777, at the age of 42.

458.

Gwinnett is buried at Colonial Park Cemetery in Savannah, Georgia.

459.

His grave was unmarked for many years until a monument was erected in his honor in 1842.

460.

Gwinnett County, Georgia, is named after Button Gwinnett and was established in 1818.

461.

Gwinnett's signature is featured on the Georgia state flag.

462.

His home, known as Gwinnett Hall, was burned down during the American Revolution and no longer exists.

463.

Gwinnett's role as a signer of the Declaration of Independence solidified his place in American history.

464.

His signature is displayed in museums and historical collections around the world.

465.

Gwinnett's reputation and contributions have been celebrated in various books, documentaries, and scholarly works.

466.

He is often portrayed as a patriot who fought for the cause of American independence.

467.

Gwinnett's life and legacy continue to be studied and examined by historians and scholars.

468.

His character and political beliefs were shaped by the Enlightenment ideals of liberty, equality, and self-governance.

469.

Gwinnett's descendants have maintained a prominent presence in Georgia's political and social landscape.

470.

His son, also named Button Gwinnett, served as the mayor of Savannah and as a state legislator.

471.

Gwinnett's great-grandson, William Gwinnett Mather, served as a U.S. Senator from Wyoming.

472.

Gwinnett's family legacy extends to the present day, with numerous descendants still residing in Georgia.

473.

The Button Gwinnett Elementary School in Peachtree Corners, Georgia, is named in his honor.

474.

Gwinnett's life and contributions to American independence are commemorated annually on Button Gwinnett Day in Georgia.

475.

Gwinnett's signature has been featured on postage stamps, currency, and various official documents.

476.

He is often depicted in historical artwork and portraits, capturing his image for future generations.

477.

Gwinnett's role as a founding father and signer of the Declaration of Independence has secured his place in American history.

478.

His commitment to the cause of liberty and independence remains an inspiration to future generations.

479.

Gwinnett's life story and achievements serve as a reminder of the sacrifices made by those who fought for the birth of the United States.

480.

He is remembered as a key figure in Georgia's history and its contribution to the American Revolution.

481.

Gwinnett's life and legacy continue to be studied and celebrated as part of the broader narrative of American independence.

482.

His story exemplifies the struggles and challenges faced by the early patriots in their quest for freedom.

483.

Gwinnett's name is often invoked in discussions of the American Revolution and the formation of the United States.

484.

His contributions to the cause of American independence, both as a political leader and military officer, are an enduring part of the nation's history.

485.

The Addax (Addax nasomaculatus) is a critically endangered species of antelope native to the Sahara Desert.

486.

It is also known as the white antelope or screwhorn antelope due to its distinctive twisted horns.

487.

Addax are well adapted to desert life, with specialized physical and physiological features.

488.

Adult Addax stand about 3 feet (1 meter) tall at the shoulder and weigh between 220 and 330 pounds (100-150 kilograms).

489.

They have a stocky build with a white or sandy-colored coat that helps them blend into their desert habitat.

490.

Male Addax have long, spiraling horns that can reach up to 3 feet (1 meter) in length.

491.

Female Addax also have horns, but they are smaller and more slender.

492.

The horns of Addax are an important defensive tool and are used during territorial disputes.

493.

These antelopes have a unique adaptation called nasal glands, which help them conserve water by reducing moisture loss during exhalation.

494.

Addax are primarily herbivores and feed on grasses, leaves, and other desert vegetation.

495.

They have the ability to extract moisture from the plants they eat, allowing them to survive in arid environments.

496.

Addax have specialized kidneys that can concentrate urine, allowing them to conserve water.

497.

These antelopes have a slow metabolism, which helps them survive in extreme heat and endure long periods without water.

498.

Addax are well-suited to their desert habitat and can tolerate temperatures exceeding 122°F (50°C).

499.

They have adapted to minimize their water requirements by obtaining moisture from the plants they consume.

500.

Addax have a unique social structure and form small groups called herds.

501.

The herds typically consist of a dominant male, several females, and their offspring.

502.

The male Addax defends his territory and mates with the females within his group.

503.

During the breeding season, male Addax engage in ritualized displays to attract females.

504.

Female Addax give birth to a single calf after a gestation period of around 9 months.

505.

Calves are able to walk and follow their mothers shortly after birth.

506.

Addax calves have a reddish-brown coat, which gradually turns white as they mature.

507.

The white coloration of adult Addax helps reflect the sun's rays and keep them cool in the desert heat.

508.

These antelopes have excellent hearing and eyesight, which helps them detect predators such as lions and hyenas.

509.

Addax are known for their remarkable ability to remain motionless for long periods, allowing them to blend in with their surroundings and avoid detection.

510.

The main predators of Addax are lions, hyenas, and humans.

511.

The population of Addax has significantly declined in recent decades
due to hunting, habitat loss, and desertification.

512.

They are classified as critically endangered by the International
Union for Conservation of Nature (IUCN).

513.

The Sahara Conservation Fund and other organizations are working
to protect and conserve Addax populations in their remaining range.

514.

Addax have been reintroduced into protected areas in Chad, Niger,
and Tunisia to help increase their numbers.

515.

They are considered a flagship species for the conservation of desert
ecosystems.

516.

Addax are also important for ecosystem functioning, as their grazing
behavior helps maintain vegetation balance in arid regions.

517.

These antelopes are well adapted to survive in harsh desert
conditions, but their numbers continue to decline due to ongoing
threats.

518.

In the wild, Addax can live up to 20 years, while in captivity, they can live for over 25 years.

519.

Addax have been historically hunted for their meat, hides, and horns, leading to their decline.

520.

The Addax is considered a symbol of beauty and grace in many African cultures.

521.

In some regions, the Addax is regarded as a sacred animal and is protected by local communities.

522.

The conservation of Addax requires efforts to combat illegal hunting and promote sustainable land management practices.

523.

These antelopes have been reintroduced to semi-captive environments, where they can be protected and managed more effectively.

524.

Conservation breeding programs are also in place to safeguard the genetic diversity of captive Addax populations.

525.

Addax have a strong association with their native desert habitat and are rarely found outside of it.

526.

They have evolved to cope with extreme heat, sandstorms, and the scarcity of water and vegetation.

527.

Addax have specially adapted hooves that help them traverse sandy and rocky terrains.

528.

These antelopes are known for their agility and speed, which they use to escape from predators.

529.

Addax are primarily active during the cooler hours of the day, such as early morning and evening.

530.

They have keen senses of smell and hearing, which aid in detecting predators and locating water sources.

531.

Addax communicate with each other using a variety of vocalizations, including snorts, grunts, and bleats.

532.

They also engage in scent marking to establish territories and communicate reproductive status.

533.

Addax have a complex digestive system that allows them to extract maximum nutrients from their food.

534.

The conservation of Addax is crucial for preserving the biodiversity and ecological balance of the Sahara Desert ecosystem.

535.

Adélie Penguins (Pygoscelis adeliae) are a species of penguin native to the Antarctic continent.

536.

They are named after the wife of French explorer Jules Dumont d'Urville, Adélie Dumont d'Urville.

537.

Adélie Penguins are known for their distinctive appearance, with a black head and back, white front, and a white ring around their eyes.

538.

They have a small, compact body with a height of about 18 to 28 inches (46 to 71 centimeters) and weigh around 8 to 13 pounds (3.6 to 5.9 kilograms).

539.

Adélie Penguins have a lifespan of approximately 10 to 20 years in the wild.

540.

They are highly adapted to the extreme Antarctic environment and have a thick layer of blubber to insulate against the cold.

541.

These penguins have a unique waddle when they walk due to their short legs and wide stance.

542.

Adélie Penguins are excellent swimmers and can reach speeds of up to 22 miles per hour (35 kilometers per hour) in the water.

543.

They are known for their impressive diving abilities, capable of diving to depths of over 500 feet (150 meters) and staying underwater for up to 7 minutes.

544.

Adélie Penguins feed primarily on krill, a small shrimp-like crustacean, which makes up around 90% of their diet.

545.

They also consume fish, squid, and other small marine creatures.

546.

Adélie Penguins are social birds and live in large colonies, sometimes consisting of thousands or even millions of individuals.

547.

The colonies serve as breeding grounds, and Adélie Penguins return to the same colony each year to mate and raise their young.

548.

They build nests out of stones and pebbles, carefully arranging them to protect their eggs and chicks from the cold ground.

549.

Adélie Penguins are known for their courtship rituals, which involve displays of flapping wings, vocalizations, and head movements.

550.

The female lays two eggs, usually a few days apart, and both parents take turns incubating them for about 35 days.

551.

Once hatched, the chicks are cared for by both parents and are kept warm and protected in the brood pouch, a fold of skin on the abdomen.

552.

Adélie Penguin chicks have a fluffy gray down coat that gradually molts into adult plumage.

553.

They grow quickly and are fed regurgitated food by their parents until they are able to hunt on their own.

554.

Adélie Penguins face numerous predators in the Antarctic, including leopard seals, killer whales, and skuas.

555.

They have evolved various defense mechanisms, such as forming tight groups or diving underwater to escape predators.

556.

Adélie Penguins are highly vocal and use a range of calls to communicate with their mates and offspring.

557.

The distinctive "braying" call of the Adélie Penguin is a common sound in Antarctic colonies.

558.

These penguins have an exceptional sense of hearing and can recognize their mate and chicks among thousands of other individuals.

559.

Adélie Penguins have been the subject of scientific study for over a century, providing valuable insights into Antarctic ecosystems and climate change.

560.

They are considered an indicator species, reflecting the health of the marine environment and the availability of food.

561.

Adélie Penguins undertake long migrations, traveling hundreds of miles between their breeding colonies and their feeding grounds.

562.

During the winter months, when the sea ice expands, some Adélie Penguins may travel as far north as the Antarctic Circle.

563.

They navigate using a combination of visual cues, the position of the sun, and the Earth's magnetic field.

564.

Adélie Penguins have been known to display "porpoising" behavior, leaping out of the water while swimming at high speeds.

565.

They have a streamlined body and wings that allow them to glide through the water with minimal resistance.

566.

Adélie Penguins are known for their curious and inquisitive nature, often approaching researchers and visitors in Antarctica.

567.

They have a complex social structure within their colonies, with established hierarchies and territorial disputes.

568.

Adélie Penguins have a high population density in their breeding colonies, with nests placed close together.

569.

They are monogamous birds and often form long-term pair bonds with their mates.

570.

Adélie Penguins have been observed engaging in "stone theft" from neighboring nests, taking stones to strengthen their own nests.

571.

These penguins have well-developed eyesight and can see clearly both in air and underwater.

572.

They have a gland near their eyes that secretes oil, which helps waterproof their feathers and keep them insulated.

573.

Adélie Penguins molt their feathers once a year, typically during the breeding season, which temporarily renders them flightless.

574.

They have a unique adaptation called "countercurrent heat exchange," where warm blood from their heart warms cold blood returning from their extremities, helping to conserve heat.

575.

Adélie Penguins have been observed using tools, such as sticks or rocks, to scratch themselves or to move objects.

576.

They have a high tolerance for extreme cold and can withstand temperatures as low as -40 degrees Fahrenheit (-40 degrees Celsius).

577.

Adélie Penguins have been studied for their navigational abilities and their ability to detect changes in their environment.

578.

They are considered a keystone species in the Antarctic ecosystem, playing a crucial role in nutrient cycling and trophic dynamics.

579.

Adélie Penguins have been featured in numerous documentaries and films, contributing to their popularity and recognition.

580.

They have been the inspiration for various works of art, literature, and children's books, capturing the hearts of people around the world.

581.

Adélie Penguins face environmental challenges, including climate change, loss of sea ice, and competition for food resources.

582.

Conservation efforts are underway to protect Adélie Penguin populations and their breeding colonies in Antarctica.

583.

Adélie Penguins are a protected species under the Antarctic Treaty System, which prohibits their disturbance or harm.

584.

Studying Adélie Penguins provides valuable insights into the impacts of climate change on polar regions and the importance of preserving these unique ecosystems.

585.

Lyman Hall (1724-1790) was an American physician, clergyman, and statesman who played a significant role in the American Revolution.

586.

He was born on April 12, 1724, in Wallingford, Connecticut, and later moved to Georgia.

587.

Hall graduated from Yale College in 1747 and then studied medicine, becoming a respected physician.

588.

He was also ordained as a Congregationalist minister but later converted to the Episcopal Church.

589.

In 1752, Hall moved to Georgia and established a successful medical practice in Savannah.

590.

Hall became involved in local politics and was elected to represent St. John's Parish in the Georgia Provincial Assembly in 1768.

591.

He was an early supporter of American independence and was elected as a delegate to the Second Continental Congress in 1775.

592.

In 1776, Hall signed the United States Declaration of Independence, representing Georgia as one of the signatories.

593.

He was the only clergyman to sign the Declaration of Independence.

594.

During the Revolutionary War, Hall served as a delegate to the Georgia state constitutional convention and as governor of Georgia from 1783 to 1784.

595.

Hall played a crucial role in the formation of the state of Georgia and was instrumental in establishing the state's legal and political systems.

596.

He was known for his strong advocacy of religious freedom and the separation of church and state.

597.

Hall was an ardent supporter of education and helped found the University of Georgia, serving on its board of trustees.

598.

He was appointed as Georgia's representative to negotiate a boundary treaty with the Creek Nation.

599.

Hall's political career continued after the war, and he served in the Georgia state legislature and as a judge of the superior court.

600.

He retired from politics in 1790 and devoted his later years to his medical practice and his family.

601.

Hall was married twice. His first wife, Mary Osborne, died in 1761, and he remarried to Elizabeth Wells in 1764.

602.

He had several children, including a daughter named Sarah who married Georgia governor George Mathews.

603.

Hall's ancestral home, Hall's Knoll, in Connecticut, is now part of a state park and is open to the public.

604.

He was known for his integrity, honesty, and strong moral character, earning him the respect and admiration of his peers.

605.

Hall was a skilled orator and a persuasive speaker, using his eloquence to advocate for the principles of liberty and independence.

606.

He was a devout Christian and believed in the importance of individual rights and freedoms.

607.

Hall's signature on the Declaration of Independence is considered one of the most elegant and distinctive among the signatories.

608.

He was one of three Georgia signers of the Declaration of Independence, along with Button Gwinnett and George Walton.

609.

Hall's support for American independence was not without personal sacrifice. His properties in Georgia were destroyed by British forces during the war.

610.

In recognition of his contributions to the founding of the United States, a monument was erected in honor of Lyman Hall in his hometown of Wallingford, Connecticut.

611.

Hall's legacy as a patriot and statesman is celebrated in Georgia, where numerous buildings, streets, and schools bear his name.

612.

He believed in the power of representative government and the importance of citizen participation in the political process.

613.

Hall's commitment to liberty and justice inspired future generations of Americans to uphold the principles he fought for.

614.

He is remembered as one of Georgia's founding fathers and a key figure in the early history of the United States.

615.

Hall's portrait is featured in the Rotunda of the United States Capitol, commemorating his role in the nation's founding.

616.

He maintained correspondence with prominent figures of his time, including Thomas Jefferson and Benjamin Rush.

617.

Hall's influence extended beyond politics and medicine. He was also a farmer and horticulturist, experimenting with new agricultural techniques.

618.

In addition to English, Hall was fluent in Latin and Greek, reflecting his classical education.

619.

Hall was known for his philanthropy and charitable works, providing financial support to various causes, including education and relief for the poor.

620.

He was a strong advocate for the rights of Native Americans and worked to promote peaceful relations between settlers and indigenous peoples.

621.

Hall's commitment to public service and his dedication to the ideals of the American Revolution earned him the admiration of his contemporaries.

622.

He was known for his humility and modesty, often downplaying his own achievements and emphasizing the collective effort of the American people.

623.

Hall's contributions to the founding of the United States were recognized posthumously when he was inducted into the Georgia Hall of Fame in 2002.

624.

He was a man of principles and stood firmly by his convictions, even in the face of opposition and adversity.

625.

Hall's advocacy for religious freedom laid the groundwork for the First Amendment's protection of freedom of religion in the United States.

626.

He was known for his meticulous record-keeping, and his papers and correspondence provide valuable insights into the history of the American Revolution.

627.

Hall's dedication to public service and his unwavering commitment to the principles of liberty continue to inspire Americans today.

628.

He believed in the power of education to transform society and played a crucial role in establishing educational institutions in Georgia.

629.

Hall's contributions to the establishment of the United States as an independent nation have earned him a place among the nation's founding fathers.

630.

He was known for his strong work ethic and his dedication to the betterment of his community and country.

631.

Hall's life and career exemplify the values of the American Revolution, including liberty, equality, and self-governance.

632.

He was a staunch supporter of the rights of the common people and fought for equal representation and fair treatment for all.

633.

Hall's commitment to public service and his tireless efforts to advance the cause of American independence have left an indelible mark on the nation's history.

634.

His life and legacy continue to be celebrated and honored as a testament to the enduring spirit of the American Revolution.

635.

African buffalos, also known as Cape buffalos or African buffalo bulls, are large bovines found in sub-Saharan Africa.

636.

They are one of the "Big Five" game animals, along with elephants, lions, leopards, and rhinoceroses.

637.

African buffalos are known for their robust build, with males weighing between 500 and 900 kilograms (1,100 and 2,000 pounds), and females weighing slightly less.

638.

They are highly social animals and form large herds that can consist of hundreds or even thousands of individuals.

639.

African buffalos have a distinctive, sturdy build with a broad chest, strong limbs, and a large head.

640.

Both males and females have large, curving horns that can grow up to 1.5 meters (5 feet) in length.

641.

The horns of male buffalos are thicker and more robust than those of females, and they use them for fighting and dominance displays.

642.

African buffalos have a dark brown or black coat, which provides camouflage and protection from the sun and insects.

643.

They have a high tolerance for heat and are well adapted to living in the African savannah and grasslands.

644.

African buffalos are herbivores and primarily feed on grasses, but they also eat leaves, bark, and other plant materials.

645.

They have a complex digestive system that allows them to extract nutrients from tough and fibrous plant matter.

646.

African buffalos are known for their powerful build and formidable strength. They are capable of charging at high speeds and can be aggressive if provoked.

647.

Despite their size and strength, African buffalos are preyed upon by lions, crocodiles, and occasionally hyenas and leopards.

648.

They have a well-developed sense of hearing and smell, which helps them detect predators and stay alert in their surroundings.

649.

African buffalos engage in a behavior known as "mobbing" when they face a threat. They form a protective circle around their young, with adults facing outward and horns ready to defend.

650.

Calves are born after a gestation period of about 11.5 months. They are precocial, meaning they can stand and walk shortly after birth.

651.

Female buffalos typically give birth to a single calf, which stays close to its mother for protection and nourishment.

652.

African buffalos have a lifespan of around 15 to 25 years in the wild, although some individuals have been known to live longer.

653.

They are known to be highly adaptable animals and can survive in a wide range of habitats, including grasslands, forests, and swamps.

654.

African buffalos are important ecosystem engineers, as their grazing patterns influence the vegetation and create open areas for other wildlife.

655.

They have a symbiotic relationship with oxpecker birds, which feed on ticks and other parasites found on their bodies.

656.

African buffalos communicate through various vocalizations, including grunts, bellows, and snorts, which help maintain social cohesion within the herd.

657.

They have a hierarchical social structure within the herd, with dominant males leading and defending the group.

658.

African buffalos engage in "wallowing" behavior, where they roll in mud or water to cool down and protect themselves from biting insects.

659.

They are known to have a good memory and can recognize individual members of their herd even after long periods of separation.

660.

African buffalos are known for their resilience and toughness. They can survive in harsh conditions and endure long periods without water.

661.

They are important prey animals for carnivores and play a crucial role in maintaining the balance of the ecosystem.

662.

African buffalos have been depicted in African folklore and are often associated with strength, courage, and resilience.

663.

They are excellent swimmers and are often found in or near water bodies, where they can cool down and escape from predators.

664.

African buffalos have been domesticated in some parts of Africa for use in agriculture and transportation.

665.

They are highly territorial and defend their grazing areas and water sources from other herds or individuals.

666.

African buffalos have a keen sense of hierarchy and use various behaviors, including head butting and horn wrestling, to establish dominance within the herd.

667.

They have a unique scent gland located between their horns, which produces a strong odor used for marking territories and signaling reproductive readiness.

668.

African buffalos are known for their strong maternal instincts. Mothers are highly protective of their young and will aggressively defend them from any threat.

669.

They have an efficient circulatory system that helps regulate body temperature, allowing them to survive in extreme heat.

670.

African buffalos have been the subject of scientific research due to their complex social behaviors and ecological importance.

671.

They are capable of reaching speeds of up to 56 kilometers per hour (35 miles per hour) when running to escape predators.

672.

African buffalos have been successfully reintroduced into several protected areas where their populations had previously declined.

673.

The conservation status of African buffalos is currently categorized as "Least Concern" by the International Union for Conservation of Nature (IUCN).

674.

They are an iconic symbol of African wildlife and are often featured in wildlife documentaries and photographs.

675.

African buffalos are known to be highly adaptable to different habitats and can thrive in both protected areas and human-dominated landscapes.

676.

They play an important role in seed dispersal, as they consume fruits and excrete the seeds in different locations, aiding in the spread of plant species.

677.

African buffalos have a specialized digestive system that allows them to extract more nutrients from low-quality forage compared to other herbivores.

678.

They are known to exhibit interesting social behaviors, such as grooming each other and engaging in playful interactions within the herd.

679.

African buffalos have been observed displaying altruistic behavior, where individuals will come to the aid of injured or distressed herd members.

680.

They have an acute sense of hearing and can detect low-frequency sounds, which helps them communicate over long distances.

681.

African buffalos are capable of adapting their feeding habits based on the availability of food resources in their environment.

682.

They have a hierarchical reproductive system, where dominant males have greater mating opportunities and access to females in estrus.

683.

African buffalos have a symbiotic relationship with cattle egrets, which perch on their backs and feed on insects stirred up by their movements.

684.

They are revered by local communities in Africa and hold cultural significance as a symbol of strength, resilience, and unity.

685.

Alexander Hamilton was born on January 11, 1755, or 1757 (the exact year is debated), in the West Indies, likely on the island of Nevis or St. Kitts.

686.

Hamilton was a Founding Father of the United States and played a crucial role in shaping the nation's early government and economy.

687.

He served as the first Secretary of the Treasury under President George Washington from 1789 to 1795.

688.

Hamilton was a prolific writer and contributed to The Federalist Papers, a collection of essays advocating for the ratification of the United States Constitution.

689.

He was an influential advocate for a strong central government and believed in a strong executive branch.

690.

Hamilton's economic policies included establishing a national bank, creating a system of tariffs and taxation, and promoting industrialization to strengthen the nation's economy.

691.

He helped establish the United States Coast Guard, which was initially known as the Revenue-Marine.

692.

Hamilton was a key figure in establishing the United States Mint, which is responsible for producing and distributing the nation's currency.

693.

He played a vital role in negotiating the Compromise of 1790, which resolved the debate over the location of the nation's capital, leading to the creation of Washington, D.C.

694.

Hamilton was a staunch supporter of a strong military and played a pivotal role in shaping the United States Army and Navy.

695.

He founded the New York Post newspaper in 1801, which is still in circulation today.

696.

Hamilton was an influential lawyer and practiced law in New York City before his political career.

697.

He was a delegate to the Constitutional Convention in 1787, where he argued for a centralized government and a stronger executive branch.

698.

Hamilton was a vocal opponent of slavery and was an early member of the New York Manumission Society, which sought to abolish slavery in the state.

699.

He was involved in a famous duel with Vice President Aaron Burr on July 11, 1804, resulting in Hamilton's death the following day.

700.

Hamilton's face is featured on the $10 bill, which was redesigned in 1928 to honor his contributions to the United States.

701.

He played a significant role in establishing the concept of judicial review through his involvement in the landmark Supreme Court case Marbury v. Madison.

702.

Hamilton was an advocate for a strong national defense and played a crucial role in the development of the United States' military capabilities.

703.

He was a skilled orator and delivered powerful speeches in support of his political beliefs.

704.

Hamilton was a prolific writer of letters, essays, and speeches, leaving behind a vast body of work that provides insight into his political and economic philosophy.

705.

He co-founded the Bank of New York, which is one of the oldest banks in the United States.

706.

Hamilton was instrumental in establishing the first national census, which took place in 1790.

707.

He was a proponent of a strong relationship between the United States and Great Britain, advocating for a closer alliance and trade partnership.

708.

Hamilton was a driving force behind the creation of the United States Military Academy at West Point, which has since become one of the nation's most prestigious military institutions.

709.

IIe was an influential voice in shaping the concept of American nationalism and promoting a unified national identity.

710.

Hamilton's economic policies and vision for the United States laid the foundation for the nation's modern financial system.

711.

EHe was an early advocate for a strong executive branch and emphasized the importance of a well-functioning government to ensure stability and progress.

712.

Hamilton played a crucial role in resolving the nation's Revolutionary War debt, helping to establish the credibility of the new government.

713.

He was a staunch supporter of the Constitution and worked tirelessly to rally support for its ratification.

714.

Hamilton's belief in a strong central government and his opposition to states' rights put him at odds with some of his contemporaries, such as Thomas Jefferson.

715.

He had a complex relationship with Thomas Jefferson, with whom he frequently clashed politically but also had a mutual respect for each other's intellect.

716.

Hamilton was a skilled financial planner and played a significant role in organizing and managing George Washington's finances.

717.

He was a founding member of the New York Society for Promoting the Manumission of Slaves, which sought to end slavery in the state.

718.

Hamilton was a prolific writer and often used pseudonyms to publish his political writings and engage in public debates.

719.

He was a strong advocate for a national currency and played a pivotal role in establishing the United States dollar as the country's official currency.

720.

Hamilton's vision for a strong, centralized government laid the groundwork for the United States to become a global economic powerhouse.

721.

He was a passionate supporter of a strong national defense and believed that a well-equipped military was crucial for safeguarding the nation's interests.

722.

Hamilton was a skilled lawyer and argued several important cases that helped shape legal precedent in the early years of the United States.

723.

He was a strong advocate for the establishment of a national debt, believing it would help establish the financial stability and creditworthiness of the new nation.

724.

Hamilton's economic policies, such as the establishment of a national bank and a system of tariffs, were highly controversial and sparked intense political debates.

725.

He was a founding member of the New York Manumission Society, which advocated for the abolition of slavery in the state of New York.

726.

Hamilton's contributions to the United States Constitution and his role in shaping the early government earned him the title of "Father of American Finance."

727.

He was an influential voice in promoting the concept of a strong federal government and was a leading proponent of the necessary and proper clause of the Constitution.

728.

Hamilton's ideas on economic policy and government administration continue to have a lasting impact on the United States' financial system and governance.

729.

He was an eloquent and persuasive public speaker, known for his ability to articulate complex ideas in a clear and compelling manner.

730.

Hamilton was a firm believer in the importance of education and played a role in establishing the New York Society for the Promotion of Useful Knowledge.

731.

He played a pivotal role in the creation of the Jay Treaty, which aimed to normalize trade relations between the United States and Great Britain.

732.

Hamilton's economic policies, including the assumption of state debts by the federal government, helped solidify the nation's credit and establish financial stability.

733.

He was a founding member of the New York Chamber of Commerce, which aimed to promote trade and economic development in the city.

734.

Hamilton's life and legacy have been the subject of numerous books, plays, and films, solidifying his status as one of the most influential figures in American history.

735.

The Eagle Historic District is located in Eagle, Colorado, a small town in the Rocky Mountains.

736.

It was established as a historic district in 1979 and is listed on the National Register of Historic Places.

737.

The district encompasses a significant portion of the town, including its main street, Broadway Street.

738.

The architecture of the buildings in the district reflects the town's history and includes a mix of Victorian, Queen Anne, and Italianate styles.

739.

The district is known for its well-preserved historic buildings, which showcase the town's mining and railroad heritage.

740.

Many of the buildings in the district date back to the late 19th and early 20th centuries.

741.

The district features a variety of commercial buildings, including banks, hotels, and stores, which were essential to the town's economic development.

742.

The Tabor Opera House, located within the district, is one of the most prominent historic landmarks and a popular venue for live performances.

743.

The district also includes residential areas with charming historic homes, some of which have been converted into bed and breakfasts.

744.

The Eagle County Historical Society operates the Chambers Park Museum within the district, showcasing the town's history through exhibits and artifacts.

745.

The district's historic buildings are characterized by their decorative facades, ornate detailing, and colorful paint schemes.

746.

The Eagle Historic District is a popular destination for history enthusiasts, architecture buffs, and visitors seeking a glimpse into Colorado's past.

747.

The district is surrounded by picturesque mountain views, adding to its overall charm and appeal.

748.

The district has been the backdrop for various movies and television shows due to its authentic historic ambiance.

749.

The town of Eagle itself was established in 1882 during the Colorado silver boom.

750.

The district is a testament to the resilience and perseverance of the town's early settlers who braved the challenges of frontier life.

751.

The district's buildings have witnessed the growth and transformation of Eagle over the years, serving as witnesses to the town's history.

752.

Several buildings within the district have been repurposed and adapted for modern use while preserving their historic character.

753.

Broadway Street, the main thoroughfare in the district, retains its original layout and adds to the district's sense of continuity and authenticity.

754.

The district hosts various events and festivals throughout the year, celebrating its history and fostering community spirit.

755.

Walking tours are available in the district, allowing visitors to explore and learn about the history and significance of each building.

756.

The district's historic charm attracts artists and photographers who capture its beauty and unique character.

757.

Many of the district's buildings have plaques or markers providing historical information and context.

758.

The district's preservation efforts have been recognized with awards and accolades from historic preservation organizations.

759.

The district serves as a living history museum, providing a tangible connection to the past for residents and visitors alike.

760.

Preservation and restoration efforts in the district have focused on maintaining the original architectural features and materials.

761.

The district's historic buildings have been the subject of architectural studies and research to document their unique characteristics.

762.

The district is a vibrant and active part of the town, with a mix of commercial, residential, and cultural activities.

763.

The district's historic structures have stood the test of time and remain a testament to the craftsmanship of the era.

764.

The district is a source of pride for the local community, and its preservation is seen as a way to honor the town's heritage.

765.

The district's proximity to outdoor recreational opportunities, including hiking, fishing, and skiing, makes it an ideal destination for adventure enthusiasts.

766.

The district's buildings have been featured in local and regional publications, showcasing their architectural significance.

767.

The district's historic character and charm contribute to the town's sense of identity and place.

768.

The district's historic buildings have been passed down through generations and hold personal stories and memories of the town's residents.

769.

The district's buildings have survived natural disasters and fires, serving as resilient symbols of the town's history.

770.

The district has inspired local artists and writers, who have incorporated its architecture and ambiance into their works.

771.

The district's historic buildings have been used as settings for weddings, adding a touch of nostalgia and romance to special occasions.

772.

The district's architecture reflects the influence of various architectural styles popular during the late 19th and early 20th centuries.

773.

The district's buildings have been maintained and restored through community efforts and collaboration between property owners and preservation organizations.

774.

The district's historic structures are a reminder of the challenges faced by the early settlers and their determination to build a thriving community.

775.

The district's architectural diversity adds visual interest and creates a unique streetscape.

776.

The district is a hub for local businesses, showcasing a mix of shops, restaurants, and galleries.

777.

The district's buildings have witnessed significant events in the town's history, including economic booms, mining strikes, and community gatherings.

778.

The district's historic buildings have been documented through photographs, providing a visual record of their evolution over time.

779.

The district's architecture reflects the changing tastes and trends of the late 19th and early 20th centuries, showcasing the evolution of architectural styles.

780.

The district is an example of successful preservation efforts that have breathed new life into historic structures and contributed to the town's revitalization.

781.

The district's historic buildings have been featured in local history books and publications, serving as educational resources for future generations.

782.

The district is an important economic driver for the town, attracting tourists and supporting local businesses.

783.

The district's buildings have been used as filming locations for historical reenactments and documentaries, adding to their cultural significance.

784.

The district's historic preservation efforts have fostered a sense of community pride and unity, creating a lasting legacy for future generations to appreciate and enjoy.

785.

African elephants are the largest land animals on Earth, with males reaching heights of up to 13 feet (4 meters) at the shoulder.

786.

They have long, curved tusks made of ivory that can grow up to 10 feet (3 meters) in length.

787.

There are two subspecies of African elephants: the African forest elephant and the African savanna elephant.

788.

African elephants are highly social animals and live in complex family groups called herds.

789.

Female elephants, called cows, are typically the leaders of the herd, while males, called bulls, are more solitary.

790.

African elephants have a lifespan of around 60 to 70 years in the wild.

791.

They have a keen sense of hearing and can communicate over long distances through low-frequency rumbles.

792.

African elephants are herbivores, primarily feeding on grasses, leaves, bark, fruits, and roots.

793.

They have a unique trunk, which is a fusion of their nose and upper lip, and can be used for breathing, smelling, drinking, and grasping objects.

794.

The trunk of an African elephant has over 100,000 muscles and is incredibly strong and dexterous.

795.

African elephants have large, fan-like ears that help regulate their body temperature and cool them down in hot climates.

796.

They are highly intelligent animals and have been observed using tools and displaying problem-solving abilities.

797.

African elephants are known for their strong maternal bonds. Female elephants in a herd assist in raising and protecting the young calves.

798.

Calves are born weighing around 200 pounds (90 kilograms) and are cared for by the entire herd.

799.

African elephants have a gestation period of around 22 months, the longest of any land animal.

800.

They have a unique way of showing affection and comfort by engaging in physical contact and touching with their trunks and tusks.

801.

African elephants play a crucial role in their ecosystems by creating water holes, clearing paths, and dispersing seeds through their dung.

802.

They are excellent swimmers and can use their trunks as snorkels while crossing rivers or swimming in deep water.

803.

African elephants have a remarkable memory and can remember long-lasting social bonds, as well as recognize and remember individuals.

804.

They have a hierarchical structure within the herd, with older and larger elephants holding higher ranks.

805.

African elephants are known for their elaborate displays of behavior, such as charging, mock-fighting, and trumpeting loudly.

806.

They are capable of producing infrasound, which is a low-frequency
sound that can travel long distances and is used for long-distance
communication.

807.

African elephants have a unique sense of empathy and have been
observed comforting distressed or injured herd members.

808.

They are highly adaptable animals and can inhabit a range of
environments, from forests and grasslands to deserts and mountains.

809.

African elephants are considered a keystone species, as their
presence and activities have a significant impact on the overall
ecosystem.

810.

They are classified as vulnerable by the International Union for
Conservation of Nature (IUCN) due to habitat loss, poaching for
ivory, and human-wildlife conflict.

811.

African elephants have distinctive, wrinkled skin that helps regulate
their body temperature and protect them from the sun.

812.

They have a massive appetite and can consume up to 300 pounds
(135 kilograms) of food per day.

813.

African elephants are known for their dust bathing behavior, which
helps them clean their skin, remove parasites, and regulate body
temperature.

814.

They have a unique set of teeth called molars, which are replaced six times throughout their lifetime.

815.

African elephants have a keen sense of smell and can detect water sources from miles away.

816.

They have specialized teeth and a unique digestive system that allows them to efficiently extract nutrients from plant matter.

817.

African elephants have been observed using their tusks as tools to dig for water, break branches, and defend themselves.

818.

They have thick, padded feet with a soft, spongy structure that helps distribute their weight and reduces noise while walking.

819.

African elephants have a complex vocal repertoire and can produce a wide range of sounds, including grunts, trumpets, roars, and rumbles.

820.

They have excellent spatial awareness and can navigate through dense forests and open savannas with ease.

821.

African elephants have a highly developed sense of touch, allowing them to manipulate objects and engage in social bonding behaviors.

822.

They have a slow reproductive rate, with females typically giving birth to one calf every 4 to 5 years.

823.

African elephants have few natural predators, with lions and crocodiles being the primary threats to young calves.

824.

They have a unique cooling mechanism known as thermoregulation, where they flap their ears to increase blood flow and dissipate heat.

825.

African elephants have been revered and depicted in various African cultures and mythologies as symbols of wisdom, strength, and power.

826.

They are the focus of numerous conservation efforts and initiatives aimed at protecting their habitats and combating illegal ivory trade.

827.

African elephants have a complex system of vocal and non-vocal communication, allowing them to convey different messages and emotions.

828.

They are capable of recognizing themselves in mirrors, a cognitive ability that is rare in the animal kingdom.

829.

African elephants have a highly developed sense of empathy and have been observed mourning the loss of a herd member.

830.

They are known for their playful behavior, often engaging in activities such as mud bathing, splashing water, and play-fighting.

831.

African elephants are excellent long-distance walkers and can travel for many miles in search of food, water, or suitable habitats.

832.

They have an impressive size difference between males and females, with males being significantly larger and heavier.

833.

African elephants have a structured social hierarchy within the herd, with dominant individuals taking on leadership roles.

834.

They are a symbol of Africa's rich wildlife heritage and serve as a flagship species for conservation efforts across the continent.

835.

John Hancock was born on January 23, 1737, in Braintree, Massachusetts (now Quincy, Massachusetts).

836.

He was one of the Founding Fathers of the United States and played a crucial role in the American Revolution.

837.

Hancock was the first person to sign the United States Declaration of Independence on July 4, 1776, and his signature is the most prominent on the document.

838.

He was elected as the President of the Second Continental Congress in 1775, making him the de facto leader of the American colonies during the early stages of the Revolution.

839.

John Hancock was a wealthy merchant and was involved in various business ventures, including shipping, trading, and smuggling.

840.

He inherited a significant fortune from his uncle, which allowed him to finance revolutionary activities and support the cause of independence.

841.

Hancock served as the Governor of Massachusetts from 1780 to 1785 and again from 1787 until his death in 1793.

842.

He was a prominent advocate for the ratification of the United States Constitution and played a key role in securing its adoption in Massachusetts.

843.

John Hancock was known for his flamboyant and extravagant lifestyle, and his name became synonymous with a bold, prominent signature.

844.

He was a staunch supporter of American independence and used his position and influence to rally support for the cause.

845.

Hancock's smuggling activities made him a target of British authorities, who sought to arrest him for smuggling goods without paying customs duties.

846.

He was a close associate of Samuel Adams and worked closely with him to organize protests and resistance against British rule.

847.

Hancock was instrumental in organizing the Boston Tea Party, a key event in the lead-up to the American Revolution.

848.

Despite his wealth and status, Hancock was deeply committed to the ideals of liberty and equality and championed the rights of the common people.

849.

He was one of the wealthiest men in New England and used his resources to fund the colonial militia and provide financial support to the Continental Army.

850.

John Hancock was a target of the British authorities during the Battles of Lexington and Concord in April 1775, and his home was ransacked by British soldiers.

851.

He played a significant role in the formation of the Massachusetts Militia, which would later become part of the Continental Army.

852.

Hancock was a charismatic and influential figure, known for his ability to rally support and inspire others with his speeches and writings.

853.

He served as a delegate to the Continental Congress from 1775 to 1780 and again from 1785 to 1786.

854.

Hancock was deeply committed to the principles of individual liberty and limited government, and he fought for the inclusion of a Bill of Rights in the United States Constitution.

855.

He was an avid patron of the arts and sciences and supported various cultural and educational institutions.

856.

Hancock was a Freemason and held several prominent positions within the Masonic Order.

857.

His signature on the Declaration of Independence became a symbol of courage and defiance against British rule.

858.

John Hancock's bold signature led to the popular saying "Put your John Hancock," which means to sign one's name.

859.

He was a close friend of George Washington and supported him during his presidency.

860.

Hancock was the first to call for a boycott of British goods in response to the Stamp Act, which imposed taxes on the American colonies.

861.

He was a proponent of religious freedom and supported the separation of church and state.

862.

Hancock played a key role in the establishment of the United States Navy and advocated for a strong naval presence to protect American interests.

863.

He was a philanthropist and made significant donations to charitable causes throughout his life.

864.

Hancock's leadership during the American Revolution earned him the respect and admiration of his peers and the American people.

865.

He was known for his elegance and fashion sense, often dressing in fine clothes and wearing elaborate wigs.

866.

Hancock's mansion in Boston, known as the Hancock Manor, was a symbol of his wealth and social status.

867.

He was an avid supporter of education and helped establish several schools and colleges in Massachusetts.

868.

Hancock served as the President of the Massachusetts Provincial Congress from 1774 to 1775, leading the colonial resistance against British rule.

869.

He was a delegate to the Constitutional Convention in 1787 and played an active role in shaping the new Constitution.

870.

Hancock was an influential figure in the formation of the Massachusetts State Constitution, which became a model for other state constitutions.

871.

He was known for his generous hospitality and hosted lavish parties and events at his mansion.

872.

Hancock's role in the American Revolution made him a target of the British, and a reward was placed on his head.

873.

He was a strong advocate for the abolition of slavery and supported efforts to end the slave trade.

874.

Hancock's death on October 8, 1793, was widely mourned, and he was buried in Boston's Granary Burying Ground.

875.

He was honored with numerous monuments and memorials, including the John Hancock Tower in Boston, which is named after him.

876.

Hancock's legacy as a champion of liberty and independence continues to inspire generations of Americans.

877.

He was a skilled orator and delivered powerful speeches that resonated with the American people.

878.

Hancock's personal fortune suffered setbacks during the Revolutionary War, as his shipping and trading businesses were disrupted.

879.

He was married to Dorothy Quincy, a prominent socialite and member of a wealthy Boston family.

880.

Hancock was a member of the Sons of Liberty, a secret society that advocated for colonial rights and resistance against British rule.

881.

He was one of the wealthiest signers of the Declaration of Independence, with an estimated net worth of around $700,000 at the time.

882.

Hancock's name is forever linked with the founding of the United States and the fight for freedom and independence.

883.

He was a prominent figure in the early years of the American Republic and helped shape the country's political and legal foundations.

884.

John Hancock's life and legacy continue to be celebrated and remembered as an important chapter in American history.

885.

Fort Glenn is located on Umnak Island in the Aleutian Islands of Alaska.

886.

It was established during World War II in 1942 as a United States Army Air Corps airfield.

887.

The purpose of Fort Glenn was to provide air defense and protect the strategically important shipping lanes in the region.

888.

It was named after Colonel Benjamin S. Glenn, a Medal of Honor recipient who served in the Spanish-American War.

889.

Fort Glenn was one of the westernmost military installations in the United States during World War II.

890.

The construction of the fort involved clearing vegetation, leveling the land, and building runways, hangars, and support facilities.

891.

The fort had three runways, with the longest measuring 7,000 feet in length.

892.

It housed aircraft such as the B-24 Liberator, P-38 Lightning, and P-40 Warhawk.

893.

The fort also had anti-aircraft batteries to defend against enemy attacks.

894.

Fort Glenn played a significant role in the defense of the Aleutian Islands during the war.

895.

It was a crucial base for conducting air patrols, reconnaissance missions, and providing air support to nearby military operations.

896.

The weather conditions in the Aleutian Islands posed a significant challenge for operations at Fort Glenn, with frequent fog, high winds, and harsh winters.

897.

The fort also served as a refueling and supply point for aircraft transiting the region.

898.

It had a support staff consisting of mechanics, engineers, administrative personnel, and other essential roles to keep the base running.

899.

The fort had barracks, mess halls, recreational facilities, and other amenities to accommodate personnel stationed there.

900.

Fort Glenn was part of the broader Aleutian Islands Campaign, which aimed to prevent Japanese forces from advancing towards North America.

901.

Japanese forces conducted air raids on Fort Glenn and other installations in the Aleutians, resulting in several casualties and damage to infrastructure.

902.

The fort played a crucial role in repelling Japanese advances and maintaining control over the Aleutian Islands.

903.

Following the end of World War II, Fort Glenn was gradually downsized and its operations were scaled back.

904.

It was eventually decommissioned in 1947 and most of the structures were dismantled or abandoned.

905.

Today, remnants of the fort can still be found on Umnak Island, including concrete foundations, runways, and debris from the war.

906.

The fort's history is preserved through photographs, documents, and artifacts that provide insights into its wartime activities.

907.

Fort Glenn is now part of the Alaska Maritime National Wildlife Refuge and is managed by the U.S. Fish and Wildlife Service.

908.

The surrounding area is home to a diverse range of wildlife, including seabirds, marine mammals, and fish.

909.

The fort's location offers breathtaking views of the surrounding landscapes, with rugged coastlines, mountains, and open seas.

910.

It serves as a reminder of the significant military engagements and sacrifices made during the Aleutian Islands Campaign.

911.

The remnants of Fort Glenn are a popular destination for history enthusiasts, military historians, and those interested in World War II.

912.

The fort's ruins and abandoned structures have an eerie and evocative atmosphere, showcasing the passage of time and the impact of conflict.

913.

Visitors to Fort Glenn can explore the remains of the runways, bunkers, and other infrastructure, providing a tangible connection to the past.

914.

The fort's location in the remote Aleutian Islands adds to its mystique, as it stands as a testament to human ingenuity and perseverance in challenging environments.

915.

Fort Glenn was designated a National Historic Landmark in 1985, recognizing its historical significance.

916.

The fort's story has been documented in books, articles, and oral histories, shedding light on the experiences of those who served there.

917.

The site offers opportunities for wildlife observation, with the chance to spot birds, marine mammals, and other creatures in their natural habitat.

918.

Fort Glenn's history is intertwined with the broader history of Alaska and its strategic importance during World War II.

919.

The fort's existence and operations represented a collaborative effort between the military, government agencies, and local communities.

920.

The men and women stationed at Fort Glenn faced numerous challenges, including extreme weather conditions, isolation, and the constant threat of enemy attacks.

921.

The fort's role in the Aleutian Islands Campaign helped to safeguard the security of the United States and its territories.

922.

The fort's legacy continues to resonate with the descendants of those who served there, preserving their stories and contributions.

923.

The ruins of Fort Glenn provide a unique backdrop for photography and artistic exploration, capturing the juxtaposition of nature and history.

924.

The fort's location in a pristine natural environment offers opportunities for outdoor activities such as hiking, fishing, and wildlife spotting.

925.

Researchers and archaeologists continue to study the remains of Fort Glenn, uncovering new insights into its construction, operations, and impact.

926.

The fort serves as a reminder of the sacrifices made by servicemen and women during times of war and the importance of preserving historical sites.

927.

The fort's strategic location in the Aleutian Islands made it a crucial outpost for monitoring and defending against potential threats.

928.

The fort's presence contributed to the overall Allied strategy in the Pacific Theater and helped maintain a secure supply line to Alaska.

929.

Fort Glenn played a role in supporting scientific research and surveying efforts in the region, providing logistical support and resources.

930.

The fort's operations required a coordinated effort across multiple military branches and support units, showcasing the importance of teamwork.

931.

The fort's proximity to the harsh Alaskan environment presented unique challenges in terms of logistics, transportation, and resource management.

932.

The legacy of Fort Glenn extends beyond its military significance, as it also served as a temporary home for personnel who formed lasting bonds and friendships.

933.

The fort's ruins have become an integral part of the natural landscape, blending with the surrounding vegetation and serving as a testament to the passage of time.

934.

Fort Glenn stands as a testament to the resilience and determination of those who served there, leaving a lasting imprint on the history and identity of the Aleutian Islands.

935.

The African Forest Elephant (Loxodonta cyclotis) is one of two subspecies of African elephants, with the other being the African Bush Elephant (Loxodonta africana).

936.

They are native to the tropical forests of Central and West Africa.

937.

African Forest Elephants are smaller than their bush counterparts, with an average shoulder height of about 8 to 10 feet (2.4 to 3 meters).

938.

They have straighter tusks compared to African Bush Elephants, and their tusks are thinner and more downward-pointing.

939.

The tusks of African Forest Elephants are highly sought after by poachers, contributing to their decline in population.

940.

These elephants play a crucial role in maintaining the biodiversity of the forest ecosystem as they disperse seeds through their dung.

941.

African Forest Elephants have a complex social structure, living in small family groups led by a matriarch.

942.

The matriarch is typically the oldest and most experienced female in the group.

943.

They communicate using a variety of vocalizations, including trumpeting, rumbling, and growling.

944.

African Forest Elephants have a keen sense of hearing and can pick up low-frequency sounds that are inaudible to humans.

945.

Their diet consists of a variety of plant material, including leaves, fruits, bark, and twigs.

946.

African Forest Elephants are known for their ability to move silently through dense forests, thanks to their padded feet and agile bodies.

947.

They have a prehensile trunk that they use for feeding, drinking, and social interactions.

948.

African Forest Elephants are excellent swimmers and often utilize water bodies in their habitat for bathing and cooling down.

949.

These elephants have long lifespans, with individuals living up to 60 years or more in the wild.

950.

Female African Forest Elephants reach sexual maturity around the age of 10 to 12 years, while males mature later, around 20 to 25 years.

951.

The gestation period for African Forest Elephants is approximately 22 months, making it one of the longest among mammals.

952.

Calves are born weighing around 200 pounds (90 kilograms) and are cared for by their mothers and other females in the group.

953.

African Forest Elephants have a well-developed sense of touch, using their trunks to explore their environment and bond with other elephants.

954.

They have thick, wrinkled skin that helps protect them from insect bites and sunburn.

955.

African Forest Elephants have been observed using tools, such as sticks, to scratch themselves or to dig for water.

956.

They are known to create clearings in the forest by pushing down trees and shrubs, shaping their environment to suit their needs.

957.

African Forest Elephants are important ecosystem engineers, influencing forest structure and promoting plant diversity.

958.

Due to their elusive nature and the dense forests they inhabit, African Forest Elephants are more difficult to study compared to their bush counterparts.

959.

Their population has declined significantly due to habitat loss, poaching for ivory, and human-wildlife conflict.

960.

African Forest Elephants are listed as Critically Endangered by the International Union for Conservation of Nature (IUCN).

961.

Conservation efforts are focused on protecting their habitat, combating illegal poaching, and raising awareness about their ecological importance.

962.

African Forest Elephants are key indicators of the health of tropical forests, as their presence is linked to forest integrity.

963.

They have a unique feeding strategy called "push-and-pull," where they use their trunks and tusks to uproot small trees and strip the bark from larger trees.

964.

African Forest Elephants have a larger brain size compared to African Bush Elephants, which is thought to be associated with their complex social behavior.

965.

These elephants are essential for the dispersal of large-seeded trees, helping to regenerate the forest.

966.

African Forest Elephants have a reddish-brown skin color, which acts as camouflage in the forest environment.

967.

They have a thick undercoat of hair that helps insulate them from temperature extremes.

968.

African Forest Elephants are highly adaptable and can survive in a range of forest types, including lowland rainforests and montane forests.

969.

They have a specialized digestive system that allows them to extract nutrients from fibrous plant material.

970.

African Forest Elephants have a slower reproduction rate compared to African Bush Elephants, which makes their population recovery more challenging.

971.

They are known for their ability to navigate through dense vegetation using their memory and spatial cognition.

972.

African Forest Elephants have a symbiotic relationship with certain bird species that feed on insects and parasites found on their bodies.

973.

These elephants are highly sensitive to disturbances in their environment, including changes in rainfall patterns and increased human activities.

974.

They play a vital role in nutrient cycling within the forest ecosystem, as their dung contributes to soil fertility.

975.

African Forest Elephants have been observed engaging in playful behavior, such as splashing in water and mock-fighting with each other.

976.

Their complex vocalizations serve various purposes, including communication within the group and maintaining social bonds.

977.

African Forest Elephants are known to visit mineral-rich salt licks, where they obtain essential minerals not readily available in their diet.

978.

They have large, fan-shaped ears that help dissipate heat and regulate body temperature in the hot and humid forest environment.

979.

African Forest Elephants are highly adaptable to changes in their habitat and have been known to exploit secondary growth forests and disturbed areas.

980.

They have a high tolerance for tannins, which are present in many of the plants they consume.

981.

African Forest Elephants have been observed using tree trunks and branches as rubbing posts, helping them remove parasites and dead skin.

982.

These elephants are capable of long-distance movements, allowing them to access different food sources and maintain genetic diversity.

983.

African Forest Elephants have been studied using satellite tracking and GPS technology to understand their movement patterns and habitat requirements.

984.

Efforts to conserve African Forest Elephants focus on protecting their remaining habitat, strengthening anti-poaching measures, and promoting sustainable land-use practices to ensure their long-term survival.

985.

The Holy Assumption Orthodox Church is an architectural gem located in a small town in a rural setting.

986.

It is a classic example of Byzantine-style architecture, characterized by its distinctive domes and ornate decorative elements.

987.

The church's construction began in the late 19th century and was completed in the early 20th century, showcasing impressive craftsmanship.

988.

The exterior of the church features intricate brickwork, ornamental details, and colorful frescoes.

989.

The interior of the church is adorned with beautiful icons, murals, and religious artifacts, providing a serene and spiritually uplifting atmosphere.

990.

The Holy Assumption Orthodox Church is a place of worship for the local Orthodox Christian community, serving as a center for religious ceremonies and events.

991.

The church's design incorporates symbolic elements, such as crosses, domes, and arches, representing the spiritual significance of the Orthodox faith.

992.

The Holy Assumption Orthodox Church serves as a cultural and historical landmark, reflecting the rich heritage and traditions of the Orthodox Christian community.

993.

The church is known for its regular religious services, including liturgies, prayers, and sacraments, attracting both locals and visitors seeking spiritual solace.

994.

The church plays an active role in the community, organizing charitable activities, educational programs, and cultural events.

995.

The Holy Assumption Orthodox Church celebrates important religious holidays and festivals, which are marked by special services, processions, and traditional rituals.

996.

The church's clergy consists of dedicated priests and deacons who guide the congregation and provide pastoral care.

997.

The church's architecture and interior design reflect the influence of the Orthodox Christian tradition, combining elements from various cultural and artistic styles.

998.

The Holy Assumption Orthodox Church stands as a testament to the faith and resilience of the Orthodox community, preserving its religious and cultural heritage.

999.

The church attracts visitors interested in religious art, history, and architecture, providing a unique glimpse into the Orthodox Christian tradition.

1000.

The Holy Assumption Orthodox Church serves as a place of spiritual retreat, where individuals can find solace, reflection, and a connection to the divine.